STRENGTH
SIGNIFICANCE. RESILIENCE. COURAGE.

Copyright © 2020 Hillsong International Ltd atf Hillsong International

Version 4

All rights reserved. No part of this book may be reproduced in any form by any mechanical or electronic means including information storage or retrieval systems, without permission in writing from the publisher.

While the manual is consistent with the values of Hillsong, the program and manual are suitable for use within any value or faith-based system. The purpose of this community development program is to promote a holistic, humanitarian and strengths-based approach to life.

Enquiries should be addressed to the publishers.

Hillsong Music Australia, PO Box 1195, Castle Hill NSW 1765, Australia

T: +61 2 8853 5300
F: +61 2 8846 4625
E: resources@hillsong.com

Warning:

The STRENGTH Facilitator Handbook and STRENGTH Journals are provided to help facilitate the running of the STRENGTH program. Although the content of the program is copyright protected it does NOT constitute, or contain legal, medical or other advice. Use of this handbook and running the program is entirely at your own risk.

Before running this program, you should obtain your own legal, insurance and other professional advice in the State, Territory or Country in which you intend to run the program.

STRENGTH
SIGNIFICANCE. RESILIENCE. COURAGE.

JOURNAL

Name

_____

Date

_____

CONTENTS

STRENGTH OVERVIEW .... *page 6*
SESSION ONE: Leave Your Mark .... *page 11*
SESSION TWO: No Man is an Island .... *page 17*
SESSION THREE: Can't Touch This .... *page 29*
SESSION FOUR: Too Tough to Get Rough .... *page 35*
SESSION FIVE: Power Balance .... *page 43*
SESSION SIX: Too Traditional for Today .... *page 51*
SESSION SEVEN: Cause & Effect .... *page 59*
SESSION EIGHT: The Man for the Dream .... *page 67*
SESSION NINE: Live the Adventure .... *page 75*

STRENGTH OVERVIEW

STRENGTH is a unique personal development and group mentoring tool that uses an inspirational, practical and experiential approach to learning. This program is founded upon the premise that every life counts and has intrinsic value, and fosters an awareness of this belief. As a result, participants are equipped to become effective global citizens for the future.

AIM For you to develop an understanding of the positive contribution you can make to the communities around you, and to know that you have **SIGNIFICANCE RESILIENCE** and **COURAGE**.

OBJECTIVES
// Identify yourself as valuable with much to contribute.
// Build confidence, self-awareness and courage.
// Develop decision-making and problem-solving skills.
// Understand you are able to have a positive influence in their world.
// Identify personal strengths and desires to motivate them to set and achieve their goals.

THESE PROGRAM OBJECTIVES ARE ACHIEVED THROUGH 3 FOUNDATIONAL CONCEPTS: SIGNIFICANCE. RESILIENCE. COURAGE.

[I HAVE]
SIGNIFICANCE
BODY AND SOUL, I AM WONDERFULLY MADE The focus for these sessions is for each participant to learn that they have a significant role to play in building positive communities and to understand for themselves that they are valuable, unique and one-of-a-kind.

RESILIENCE
CHOOSE LIFE These sessions explore the power of choice and the impact your decisions have on shaping your future. This is addressed through practical sessions exploring resilience, respect, emotions, decision-making and problem-solving.

COURAGE
I HAVE A HOPE AND A FUTURE Being courageous is examined through exploring your hopes, dreams, desires, attitudes towards relationships and risk-taking behaviours. Goal setting, group discussions and practical activities are used to explore these topics.

SIGNIFICANCE

SESSION ONE LEAVE YOUR MARK **SESSION TWO** NO MAN IS AN ISLAND

[BODY AND SOUL, I AM WONDERFULLY MADE]

[BODY AND SOUL, I AM WONDERFULLY MADE]

1
SIGNIFICANCE
SESSION ONE LEAVE YOUR MARK

OUTCOMES
BY THE END OF THIS SESSION YOU WILL BE ABLE TO:

Gain an understanding of the purpose of the course.
Develop an awareness of personal value and identity.

FOUNDATIONAL CONCEPTS

SIG·NIF·I·CANCE *[SIG-NIF-I-KUHNS]* The quality of being worthy of attention; importance.

U·NIQUE *[YOO-NEEK]* A one-off, original, exceptional, rare, unequalled, extraordinary, incomparable, matchless, individual.

"Our lives are valuable. We are one-of-a-kind individuals. Who we are is irreplaceable. There is a reason for our existence. We are not rubbish. We are not a mistake. We are made with purpose.

Human life is valuable; it is the most precious commodity on earth. People's lives hold far greater value than fame or material wealth. An individual's value has nothing to do with what we think or what people say about us. Our value is not related to what we do and it is not based on our circumstances, family background, religion or how much money we have. Value can't be earned; nothing can change how valuable we are. Because we are valuable, we are worthy of being treated well and this starts with us, valuing ourselves means looking after ourselves.

We are unique; there is no-one else the same as us. How we are designed, our passions, our talents, our strengths are unique to each of us and have purpose. All these qualities are in us so we can fulfil our future. We are purpose-built and exist for a reason. There is a purpose for our lives."

"BE YOU... EVERYONE ELSE IS ALREADY TAKEN" // AUTHOR UNKNOWN

"WHY COMPARE YOURSELF WITH OTHERS? NO ONE IN THE ENTIRE WORLD CAN DO A BETTER JOB OF BEING YOU THAN YOU" // AUTHOR UNKNOWN

ILLUSTRATION: CAR
IF YOU WERE GIVEN A REALLY EXPENSIVE CAR

// How would you treat your new car?
// Where would you park it?
// Who would you let drive it?
// Would you drive it through rough terrain?
// Would you put premium petrol instead of normal unleaded petrol?
// Would you get it regularly serviced and cleaned?

HOW WE TREAT SOMETHING DEPENDS ON HOW VALUABLE WE THINK IT IS. EACH OF US IS PRICELESS AND EACH OF US IS OF HIGH WORTH AND VALUE. BECAUSE WE ARE VALUABLE, WE DESERVE TO BE TREATED WELL AND WITH RESPECT.

REFLECTION

Q. If you could be anyone, who would you be?

_____

_____

Q. Why would you want to be anyone else other than you?

_____

_____

_____

_____

Q. What have you learnt about yourself today?

_____

_____

_____

_____

Take some time this week to think about what you like to do and why you like doing it. For example, if you like football, why do you like it? It could be that you enjoy comradery. This is part of the discovery of our personal identity.

[BODY AND SOUL, I AM WONDERFULLY MADE]

2
SIGNIFICANCE
SESSION TWO NO MAN IS AN ISLAND

OUTCOMES
BY THE END OF THIS SESSION YOU WILL BE ABLE TO:

Explore the value of friendship.
Discover the benefits of teamwork.

FOUNDATIONAL CONCEPT

SIG·NIF·I·CANCE *[SIG-NIF-I-KUHNS]* The quality of being worthy of attention; importance.

U·NIQUE *[YOO-NEEK]* A one-off, original, exceptional, rare, unequalled, extraordinary, incomparable, matchless, individual.

We are unique; there is no one else who is the same as us. How we are designed, our passions, our talents, and our strengths are unique to each of us and have purpose. All these qualities are in us so we can fulfil our future. We are purpose-built and exist for a reason. There is a purpose for our lives.

What we do with our life is unique to our individual make-up. Our contribution to the world is significant because only we can make it. We can all do something and be someone of significance.

You are the only YOU there can BE. There is no one else like you. There is something in you that the world needs. You can leave your mark by making a positive contribution to the communities around you!

"BE YOU... EVERYONE ELSE IS ALREADY TAKEN" // AUTHOR UNKNOWN

"WHY COMPARE YOURSELF WITH OTHERS? NO ONE IN THE ENTIRE WORLD CAN DO A BETTER JOB OF BEING YOU THAN YOU" // AUTHOR UNKNOWN

REFLECTION

Q. What is a true friend?

_____
_____
_____
_____
_____
_____
_____

Q. Why do we need community?

_____
_____
_____
_____
_____
_____
_____

Q. What do you value in friendships?

___

Q. What qualities make a good friend?

___

Q. What do these qualities look like practically, in a friendship?

True friends will 'sharpen' you (i.e. Challenge you, push you forward, encourage you to be the best you can be, and tell you what you may not want to hear but do so because they have your best interests at heart). Friends that can listen to you and give you constructive advice.

_____
_____
_____
_____
_____
_____
_____

Q. What friendships are important for you to develop in the future?

_____
_____
_____
_____
_____
_____
_____
_____

Q. Have you ever done anything you would not have normally done because of a friends encouragement, that had a positive impact?

_____
_____
_____
_____
_____
_____
_____
_____

Q. What can you do practically this week to create a new friendship or build on an existing one?

_____
_____
_____
_____
_____
_____
_____
_____

Q. What did you like about working in a team today?

_____
_____
_____
_____
_____
_____
_____

Q. How can you be UNIQUELY YOU?

- Be confident that you can positively contribute
- Put yourself out there, try new things, and discover what is in you
- Choose to be kind to others

_____
_____
_____
_____
_____
_____
_____
_____
_____
_____
_____
_____

NOTES

RESILIENCE

SESSION THREE CAN'T TOUCH THIS **SESSION FOUR** TOO TOUGH TO GET ROUGH
SESSION FIVE POWER BALANCE

[CHOOSE LIFE]

[CHOOSE LIFE]

3
RESILIENCE
SESSION THREE CAN'T TOUCH THIS

OUTCOMES
BY THE END OF THIS SESSION YOU WILL BE ABLE TO:

Recognise the value of developing resilience.

FOUNDATIONAL CONCEPT
RE·SIL·IENCE *[RI-ZIL-YUHNS, -ZIL-EE-UHNS]* Ability to recover readily from adversity

Resilience is the strength to withstand adversity. It is the ability to handle difficult situations, people, environments and setbacks. It is key to overcoming life's challenges, temptations and adversity. Being able to bounce back and recover from adversity makes us stronger and contributes to our dreams becoming a reality. Young people can have incredible resilience. They can continually surprise us with their ability to bounce back rather than giving in to circumstances.

A resilient person is able to stand firm whilst facing significant difficulties and stress, as they have a strong sense of self-belief and faith in their capabilities.

We need to understand that life will not always be smooth sailing. Life is not always great. Things happen that we would prefer didn't. But if life was always wonderful, would we appreciate all the great things or would we take them for granted? We can learn so much about ourselves when we go through challenges and problems. It is never comfortable when you're in the middle of adversity or challenge, but as you work through it you can look back and see what you have learnt from the situation.

Q. Where have I persevered?

REFLECTION

List of positive achievements I have accomplished:

1. _____
2. _____
3. _____
4. _____
5. _____
6. _____
7. _____
8. _____

List of difficult situations I have overcome:

1. _____
2. _____
3. _____
4. _____
5. _____
6. _____
7. _____
8. _____

[CHOOSE LIFE]

4
RESILIENCE
SESSION FOUR TOO TOUGH TO GET ROUGH

OUTCOMES
BY THE END OF THIS SESSION YOU WILL BE ABLE TO:

Understand anger and why we feel it.
Identify healthy ways to display anger.

FOUNDATIONAL CONCEPT

RE·SIL·IENCE *[RI-ZIL-YUHNS, -ZIL-EE-UHNS]* The ability to return to the original position or form after being compressed, bent, or stretched

Resilience is the strength to withstand adversity; it is the ability to handle difficult situations, people, environments and setbacks. It helps in overcoming life's challenges, temptations and adversity. Being able to bounce back and recover from adversity make us stronger and contributes to our dreams becoming a reality. Young people can have incredible resilience. They can continually surprise us with their ability to bounce back rather than giving in to circumstances. A resilient person is able to stand firm whilst facing significant difficulties and stress, as they have a strong sense of self-belief and faith in their capabilities.

DECISIONS WE MAKE DON'T JUST AFFECT OUR LIFE; THEY ALL IMPACT THE PEOPLE AROUND US. CHOICES CAN BE SELFISH OR SELFLESS. EVERY DECISION WE MAKE HAS A CONSEQUENCE. OFTEN WE DON'T REALISE THAT IT'S THE SMALL, EVERYDAY DECISIONS THAT CAN HAVE A PROFOUND IMPACT ON OUR FUTURE.

Q. How do you understand resilience?

_____
_____
_____
_____
_____

Q. What are some areas in life you've had to display resilience in? (eg. Being dropped from the football team, failing an exam, moving house).

_____
_____
_____
_____
_____
_____

HEALTHY & UNHEALTHY ANGER

We are going to explore healthy and unhealthy ways of dealing with anger.

HEALTHY ANGER

Healthy anger is where we don't allow anger to control us but choose to let our anger out in a way that does not cause harm to others or ourselves. Some healthy ways to work through our anger is by:
- *Responding* to a situation, not *reacting.*
- Talking to a trusted adult such as a parent or guardian; a counsellor from a school or youth helpline."
- Looking at the facts and keeping perspective.
- Doing some moderate exercise such as going outdoors for a walk/run or playing a sport that can be enjoyed with friends.
- Giving ourselves 'time out' to calm down before working through the issue.

Notes:

___

___

___

___

___

___

___

___

UNHEALTHY ANGER

Unhealthy anger is where we make wrong choices because of the anger that we feel which can cause harm to others and/or ourselves, such as violence. Some forms of unhealthy anger are:

STRATEGY	HOW WELL DOES THIS SOLVE THE PROBLEM?	HOW WOULD YOU FEEL STRAIGHT AWAY?	HOW WOULD YOU FEEL AFTER A DAY?
Screaming or Yelling			
Violence Towards Others or Ourselves			
Sulking			
Manipulation			
Trying To Control Others			
Bullying			
Emotional Blackmail*			

*People who withhold love/affection to get what they want.

REFLECTION

Q. If you feel angry this week, what strategies will you put in place to make right choices?

[CHOOSE LIFE]

5
RESILIENCE
SESSION FIVE POWER BALANCE

OUTCOMES
BY THE END OF THIS SESSION YOU WILL BE ABLE TO:

Identify ways to display respect to others and themselves.

FOUNDATIONAL CONCEPT
RE·SIL·IENCE *[RI-ZIL-YUHNS, -ZIL-EE-UHNS]*
The ability to return to the original position or form after being compressed, bent, or stretched.

RE·SPECT *[RI-SPEKT]* Esteem for or a sense of the worth or excellence of a person; the condition of being esteemed or honoured; to show regard or consideration for.

In an ideal world respect is something that we would extend to everyone. It is how we should act. Respect is something that shouldn't have to be earned, but given freely.

If we don't respect ourselves, it is difficult for us to respect others and others to respect us. Treat others the way you would like to be treated. When we respect ourselves, we tend not to willingly put ourselves in a position where we are disrespected. This is because we value ourselves. *For example:* because I respect myself, I will value my body by looking after it through regular exercise and healthy eating.

We won't always get treated the way we should, but we can choose to treat other people with respect.

REFLECTION

Q. How can we respect our friends, parents, family, and people from different cultures, religions, races or linguistic backgrounds?

Q. What are some ways that we can respect ourselves?

___

ALL PEOPLE SHOULD RECEIVE RESPECT NO MATTER HOW DIFFERENT THEY ARE TO YOU.

COURAGE

SESSION SIX TOO TRADITIONAL FOR TODAY **SESSION SEVEN** CAUSE & EFFECT
SESSION EIGHT THE MAN FOR THE DREAM

[I HAVE A HOPE AND A FUTURE]

[I HAVE A HOPE AND A FUTURE]

COURAGE
SESSION SIX TOO TRADITIONAL FOR TODAY

OUTCOMES
BY THE END OF THIS SESSION YOU WILL BE ABLE TO:

Develop understanding of a healthy relationship.
Explore how to treat people with respect and dignity.

FOUNDATIONAL CONCEPT

COUR·AGE *[KUR-IJ, KUHR-]* The quality of mind or spirit that enables a person to face difficulty; bravery Courage gives us the ability to stand up for what is right.

CON·VIC·TION *[KUHN-VIK-SHUHN]* A fixed or firm, strong belief.

A conviction helps us make decisions, especially decisions that are important and significant. Convictions produce in us the ability to act with courage. Our convictions demonstrate what we value in life.

Fear is required for courage to exist. Courage can only be expressed in the company of fear. We can use our fears to exercise courage and through that, we can discover something within us that we didn't know we had.

Acting courageously highlights that we are not fearful of what other people will say or do about the decision or stand we are making. Courage allows us to not conform to the norm. Courage allows us to face our fears or opposition without backing down, acting on what is right.

UNDERSTANDING HEALTHY RELATIONSHIPS
Q. What are some examples of someone being courageous?

Q. What do you think are admirable qualities in a person?

Q. What is one quality of a healthy relationship that is important to you?

REFLECTION
Q. How can you place value on a person in your world?

[I HAVE A HOPE AND A FUTURE]

7
COURAGE
SESSION SEVEN CAUSE & EFFECT

OUTCOMES
BY THE END OF THIS SESSION YOU WILL BE ABLE TO:

Gain understanding of the difference between healthy and unhealthy risk-taking.
Identify consequences of healthy and unhealthy risk-taking.

FOUNDATIONAL CONCEPT

COUR·AGE *[KUR-IJ, KUHR-]* The quality of mind or spirit that enables a person to face difficulty; bravery Courage gives us the ability to stand up for what is right. We need convictions to identify what it is we stand for.

CON·VIC·TION *[KUHN-VIK-SHUHN]* A fixed or firm, strong belief.

A conviction helps us make decisions, especially decisions that are important and significant. Convictions produce in us the ability to act with courage. Our convictions demonstrate what we value in life.

Fear is required for courage to exist. Courage can only be expressed in the company of fear. We can use our fears to exercise courage and through that, we can discover something within us that we didn't know we had.

Acting courageously highlights that we are not swayed by what other people will say or do about the decision or stand we are making. Courage allows us to not conform to the norm. Courage allows us to face our fears or opposition without backing down, acting on what is right.

Courage can help us to identify healthy risks and face challenges that grow and stretch us. *For example:* the number 1 fear for many people is public speaking. Developing courage to address the fear of public speaking could allow a person to see that they may be gifted in that area.

Q. What do you think are risk-taking activities?

_____
_____
_____
_____
_____
_____
_____

Q. What types of risks have positive consequences and what types of risks have negative consequences?

Risks with positive consequences: _____
_____
_____
_____
_____

Risks with negative consequences: _____
_____
_____
_____
_____

Q. Why do we need boundaries?

_____

_____

Boundaries are there to stop us from hurting others or ourselves. They keep us safe and can protect us. Boundaries create security, freedom and provide direction.

Q. What is the effect of having no boundaries?

_____

_____

_____

HEALTHY LIFESTYLE CHOICES – FITNESS AND HEALTHY EATING

Q. What are the benefits of being active? *(See some examples on the next page.)*

THE BENIFITS OF BEING ACTIVE

BEN·E·FIT *[BEN-UH-FIT]* To do good to; be of service to; something that is advantageous

// Having fun with friends and making new ones
// Opportunity for new skills and challenges
// Boost of confidence
// Bones and muscle mass get stronger
// Improved posture
// Maintenance of healthy weight
// Improved fitness
// Improves the health of your heart
// Helps you relax
// Reduces stress

[I HAVE A HOPE AND A FUTURE]

8
COURAGE
SESSION EIGHT THE MAN FOR THE DREAM

OUTCOMES
BY THE END OF THIS SESSION YOU WILL BE ABLE TO:

Recognise the importance of goal setting to achieve a dream or goal.

FOUNDATIONAL CONCEPT

COUR·AGE *[KUR-IJ, KUHR-]* The quality of mind or spirit that enables a person to face difficulty; bravery.

Every individual was created for a purpose in a specific time in history. Everyone has a sense of purpose attached to their life. No one was created by mistake. Everyone has a reason for their existence. It is up to us to find out that reason or purpose for our existence.

No matter what we do in life, we can live with an understanding that we are made for a purpose.

Fear is required for courage to exist. Courage can only be expressed in the company of fear. We can use our fears to exercise courage and through that, we can discover something within us that we didn't know we had.

Acting courageously highlights that we are not swayed by what other people will say or do about the decision or stand we are making. Courage allows us to not conform to the norm. Courage allows us to face our fears or opposition without backing down, acting on what is right.

Courage can help us to identify healthy risks and face challenges that grow and stretch us. For example: the number 1 fear for many people is public speaking. Developing courage to address the fear of public speaking could allow a person to see that they may be gifted in that area. Courage helps us develop new skills and learn new things about ourselves.

FEAR OF FAILURE CANNOT BE A GOOD ENOUGH REASON NOT TO TRY.

IMAGINE

[BIRTHDAY SPEECHES]
Imagine it is your birthday. What would you like people to say about you for your birthday speech?
What would you like people to write about you on your birthday card?

[LIKES]
If you had the total approval and admiration of everyone, regardless of what you do,
what would you do with your life?

[ROLE MODELS]
What role models do you look up to? Who inspires you?
What personal strengths or qualities do they have that you admire?

[CHARACTER STRENGTHS]
What personal strengths and qualities do you already have?
Which ones would you like to develop? How would you like to apply them?

[WEALTH]
Imagine you win the lottery or inherit a fortune. How would you spend it?
Who would you share it with?

EXAMPLE OF
A TIMELINE TO ACHIEVE A GOAL

FINISH MY EDUCATION

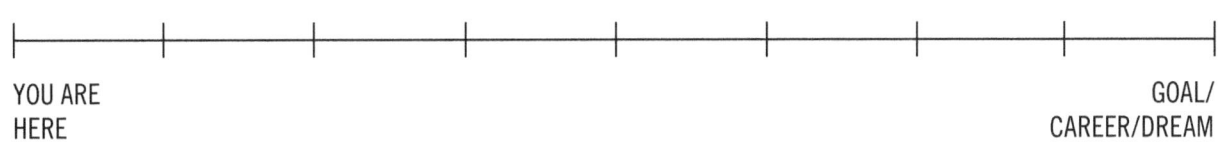

YOU ARE HERE

GOAL/ CAREER/DREAM

Each notch represents a step to take / thing to action in order to achieve desired goal.

REFLECTION

There are certain character traits and qualities we need, to help us achieve our dreams. Here are some examples:
- Hard work
- Respect
- Working together (you never know who you will meet that will help you get to where you want to go)
- Initiative / trying new things
- Confidence

Q. Can you think of other character traits and qualities we need, to help us achieve our dreams?

_____

_____

_____

_____

_____

_____

_____

PRINCIPLES FOR LIVING YOUR POTENTIAL

PO·TEN·TIAL *[PUH-TEN-SHUHL]* Capable of being or becoming

// Believe it is possible YES → GOAL → ACTION PLAN
// Work hard and persevere
// Don't get discouraged by failure
// Be confident
// Confidence brings great reward

WATCH OUT FOR DREAM STEALERS

STEAL *[STEEL]* To take without permission or right, especially secretly or by force

// Fear
// Drugs or alcohol
// Self-doubt
// Distraction
// Negative comments
// Lack of confidence

[I HAVE A HOPE AND A FUTURE]

9
COURAGE
SESSION NINE LIVE THE ADVENTURE

OUTCOMES
BY THE END OF THIS SESSION YOU WILL BE ABLE TO:

Describe what you have learnt from the program.
Participate in a team building activity.

FOUNDATIONAL CONCEPT
COUR·AGE *[KUR-IJ, KUHR-]* The quality of mind or spirit that enables a person to face difficulty; bravery.

REFLECTION
Q. What are three things that you have learnt from the STRENGTH program that you will implement in your life over the next four weeks?

NOTES

NOTES

www.ingramcontent.com/pod-product-compliance
Lightning Source LLC
Chambersburg PA
CBHW080808300426
44114CB00020B/2873